A CALL TO SERVE

BUILDING DEEPER FAITH

wesleyan PUBLISHING HOUSE
wphstore.com

Published by Wesleyan Publishing House
Indianapolis, Indiana 46250
Printed in the United States of America
ISBN: 978-0-89827-970-2
ISBN (e-book): 978-0-89827-971-9

Portions of this book have been revised from these previously published books from Wesleyan Publishing House: *Reflecting Christ* and *Connecting to Christ*.

CONTENTS

For a free group leader's guide,
visit www.wphresources.com/building.

INTRODUCTION

Welcome to an exciting journey into deeper discipleship!

This book is part of the Building Deeper Faith series, offering believers at various levels a great opportunity for deeper spiritual growth. The entire series has been developed to help you grow as a disciple of Jesus Christ. By participating in this study with others (ideally in a group), you can discover and experience how God will shape your life according to his Word, especially by using spiritual disciplines such as Bible study, prayer, Scripture memorization, and journal writing.

THE GOAL: DISCIPLESHIP

Discipleship is the life-long process of spiritual development for those who commit their lives to following Jesus. It is far more about what it means to know and follow the person of Jesus Christ than merely gaining knowledge about him. So throughout this series, the strategy for making disciples will be measured in terms of how to build in relation to others—in relation to God, to his people, and to neighbors. This time-tested strategy is built upon four core biblical values, which will be developed and explored throughout this series: sharing love, shaping lives, serving, and sending.

In your life, having discovered Christ, you no doubt are finding that you want to grow in your knowledge of him. You want to shape your life according to his Word to be his disciple. As you do, you will discover a personal ministry, a way to use your spiritual gifts to serve others. Then, having been filled with compassion for others, you will be moved to go out into the world beyond your church walls, fulfilling the Great Commission by making new disciples, thus completing the cycle of discipleship.

THE PROCESS: BUILDING DEEPER FAITH

The aim of the Building Deeper Faith series is to form disciples according to the Great Commandment and the Great Commission. The construction process of such faith can be organized around five categories: (1) foundational truths, (2) life practices, (3) virtues, (4) core values, and (5) mission.

Foundational Truths

Building Deeper Faith is based on foundational truths that are key elements for life transformation. These biblical concepts encompass the scope of Christian thinking and are always at the heart of Christian love. Learning these concepts and how they help us love God and our neighbors well will help us grow in our faith.

Life Practices

All believers must move from theory to practice. That is, we must learn to apply biblical truth to life. The practices identified in Building Deeper Faith will help us see and become open to God's work in and through us, providing the evidence of the change he is making in our lives.

Virtues

Virtues are Christlike qualities that emerge in the lives of those who are alive in Christ. Virtues replace thoughts and attitudes that come all too naturally to us whenever we are living independently from God—that is, when we are living in sin. The virtues that God's Spirit creates in us (also known in Scripture as the fruit of the Spirit) reveal the developing character into which he is transforming us, and it is what God's Spirit uses to attract others to Christ.

Core Values

Biblical truth must be applied in the framework of Christ's body, the church. The core values are the guiding principles by which the church should function in love. They are our method of operating lovingly toward God and our neighbors—they describe how and why we do the things we do.

Mission

Ultimately, believers called to love are to serve. Our mission describes what it is that we do for Christ. Each biblical truth finds a practical expression in our work.

YOUR INVOLVEMENT: SPIRITUAL DISCIPLINES

Growing disciples discover something exciting and transformational in Christian worship. The worship service is the point of entry to most churches. Yet as important as worship is, believers need more in order to grow deeper in their faith. In fact, we all long for deeper relationships.

Wouldn't it be great if there were a place we could go to make friends and find answers? Wouldn't it be wonderful if we could discover a forum to open our hearts, grow in the faith, and find unconditional love?

There is such a place—your study group!

Discipleship groups provide exactly what is needed for building deeper faith. This is because discipleship goes far beyond knowledge or even worship—it can only be meaningful as God designed in the context of loving relationships.

Just as the New Testament church was built up on teaching and preaching (Acts 5:42), so today's church must be built up by Bible study. But the key is that faith is gained. Knowledge that builds faith is ideally found in fellowship with other believers. Being connected to spiritual family as we learn makes a world of difference between mere academic knowledge acquisition and authentic discipleship.

Every believer needs a protected environment in which to discover and practice his or her faith. If you want to grow and become more effective in Christ, then find and commit to a discipleship group in which you can grow in him.

Within the context of a discipleship group, there are several simple disciplines that God's Spirit often uses powerfully in the spiritual formation of his people. Consider just these few disciplines as you seek to grow deeper in your love for God through the study of this book.

Bible Reading and Study

The Building Deeper Faith series is designed to direct you to the Bible at every point in your study. Each chapter begins with a few important Scripture passages and includes several Bible references to explore. You can enhance your study by using a good Bible translation, written in today's language.

Scripture Memorization

Memorization is a simple way to gain ownership of important passages. Each of the chapters in this book includes a key verse to memorize. This too-often-ignored discipline is a powerful tool to help you gain confidence in your knowledge of Scripture and in hearing God speak to you.

Daily Prayer and Reflection

Time alone with God is perhaps the single most important spiritual practice for any disciple. Try to spend time in prayer and reflection every day.

Personal Spiritual Journal Writing

Journal writing is a way to enhance time spent in prayer and reflection. Recording observations about your life and faith will help you process what you are learning and clarify the spiritual issues in your life. Take this study as your opportunity to begin the practice of journal writing. You'll be glad you did.

May God richly bless you and draw you closer in knowledge and love for him as you study and fellowship together with his people in your pursuit of authentic discipleship by building deeper faith.

WEEK 1

RELINQUISH CONTROL TO YOUR LORD

But our citizenship is in heaven. And we eagerly await a Savior from there, the Lord Jesus Christ, who, by the power that enables him to bring everything under his control, will transform our lowly bodies so that they will be like his glorious body.

—Philippians 3:20–21

BIBLE BASICS

- Matthew 6:24
- John 1:1–3
- John 11:27
- Romans 13:14

List several words that describe Jesus, based on the above Scriptures. How is this description the same or different from what you thought about Jesus before now?

WE ARE CALLED TO SURRENDER

The situation seemed hopeless. Encircled by the enemy, low on supplies and ammunition, and enduring relentless bombardment and bitter cold, the men of the United States 101st Airborne Division faced starvation or annihilation. It was December 1944. The place was Bastogne, France. The German army had launched the winter offensive that became known as the Battle of the Bulge, a clash that overwhelmed American troops in the thinly defended Ardennes forest. Bastogne was surrounded.

At 11:30 a.m. on December 22, the German commander offered American general A. C. McAuliffe a simple proposition: surrender and live.

What would you have done?

Outnumbered, overmatched, and undersupplied, the American commander shot back a one-word reply that has become a classic symbol of defiance. He said, "Nuts."

That response rallied American troops during the Second World War, and it epitomizes the modern person's independent spirit. "Nobody tells me what to do. No matter how hopeless the situation, I will be master of my fate. I will never surrender—and *nuts* to anyone who tries to make me!"

Undeniably, we are free people. God made us that way. We each were born with a free will. We are free to accept God's grace or to reject it. Not even God will compel us to do what we choose not to do.

Yet that independent attitude, so laudable as a civic principle, produces tragic results as a personal doctrine. Unlike the heroic defenders of Bastogne, those who live by a code of radical individuality may endure bitter consequences. Personal failure, broken relationships, and ruined marriages too often result from a worldview that selfishly asserts "me first." Freedom becomes slavery for many who are burdened with addictive behaviors, the result of their inability to master their desire to do whatever they please.

Into the chaos of our personal freedom, Jesus Christ issues the call to surrender—to surrender our lives to him and to accept his mastery over the world, the church, and ourselves. Though we are free, he asks that we become servants who submit to his lordship over our lives.

That notion—the lordship of Christ—is challenging for many Christians. We cherish independence as our highest ideal. We're reluctant to surrender our freedom to anyone—an employer, the church, or even Christ himself.

Yet Christ *is* Lord, and we will experience happier and more contented lives if we acknowledge that fact.

Is Christ your Lord? Have you surrendered your life to him? Let's find out what lordship means and why it's so important in our lives.

How important is your freedom? List the areas of your life that you feel sure you'd never surrender to anyone. Some examples might be your career, relationships, or finances.

CHRIST IS LORD

It's interesting to read the titles that some political leaders have given themselves. The Queen of England is officially known as "Elizabeth II, by the Grace of God of the United Kingdom of Great Britain and Northern Ireland and of Her other Realms and Territories Queen, Head of the Commonwealth, Defender of the Faith." Her son is titled "His Royal Highness Prince Charles Philip Arthur George, Prince of

Wales, Earl of Chester, Duke of Cornwall, Duke of Rothesay, Earl of Carrick, Baron of Renfrew, Lord of the Isles and Great Steward of Scotland."

Well it *sounds* impressive.

We know, however, that royals now serve a largely ceremonial function. In most cases, they have impressive titles but little or no power. They are kings and queens in name only. That's not true of Jesus. He is Lord in fact as well as in name. He is the Lord of all.

TITLES FOR JESUS

Scripture	Title
Isaiah 9:6	Mighty God
Isaiah 9:6	Prince of Peace
Isaiah 9:6	Everlasting Father
Matthew 26:63–65	Son of Man
Mark 1:2–3	Lord
Mark 8:29	The Mission
John 1:1–3	The Word (is God)
Acts 2:21 (Joel 2:32)	Lord (God)

He Is Lord of Creation

Have you ever thought about how the world was created? We may accept the fact that God did create the world, but how? By what means?

Genesis tells us that God *spoke* the world into existence. "And God *said*, 'Let there be light,' and there was light" (Gen. 1:3, emphasis added). God created the world by his word, speaking it into existence.

The New Testament tells us more about that. According to John the apostle, Jesus was the *Word* that created the world. John 1:1–3 says, "In the beginning was the Word, and the Word was with God, and the Word was God. He was with God in the beginning. Through him all things were made; without him nothing was made that has been made."

The apostle Paul echoed that thought in his letter to Christians at Colossae: "The Son is the image of the invisible God, the firstborn over all creation. For in him all things were created: things in heaven and on earth, visible and invisible, whether thrones or powers or rulers or authorities; all things have been created through him and for him" (Col. 1:15–16).

Jesus, the Word of God, was the agent of creation. He created all that exists.

And there's more. Paul wrote, "He is before all things, and in him all things hold together" (Col. 1:17). Jesus is also the sustainer of the world. He keeps it spinning and gives order and purpose to everything that exists.

He Is Lord of Salvation

Jesus is also the Christ. *Christ* is a title, not a name. It means "anointed one" and indicates that Jesus was chosen by God to save the world. This title, derived from the Greek word *christos*, parallels the Old Testament term *messiah*.

The Old Testament predicted that God would send an anointed one to his people (see 1 Sam. 2:35; Ps. 2:2; Dan. 9:25). The New Testament makes it clear that Jesus is that anointed one, the Christ. When Andrew the apostle met Jesus, he said, "'We have found the Messiah' (that is, the Christ)" (John 1:41). The apostle Peter preached that "God has made this Jesus, whom you crucified, both Lord and Messiah" (Acts 2:36). And Jesus declared himself to be the Christ (see John 4:25–26).

Jesus was no ordinary person. He was God's Anointed One who came to save the world. He proved it by his resurrection from the dead, as the apostle Paul said in Romans 1:4, "Through the Spirit of holiness [he] was appointed the Son of God in power by his resurrection from the dead: Jesus Christ our Lord."

Because this is true, there is no possibility of salvation without Jesus. Paul wrote, "If you declare with your mouth, 'Jesus is Lord,' and believe in your heart that God raised him from the dead, you will be saved" (Rom. 10:9). Jesus is God's appointed one for bringing salvation to the world. He is the Christ.

ATTRIBUTES OF JESUS

Matthew 28:18	Has universal power
Matthew 28:20	Is omnipresent
Mark 2:5–7	Has authority to forgive
John 1:1	Eternally exists
John 5:21	Can raise the dead
John 5:22, 27	Judges humankind
John 20:28	Is worshiped
Colossians 1:16	Created the world
Colossians 1:17	Sustains the world

He Is Lord of the Church

Although Jesus is now in heaven with the Father, he continues to be our Lord. Paul said, "He is the head of the body, the church; he is the beginning and the firstborn from among the dead, so that in everything he might have the supremacy" (Col. 1:18; see also Eph. 5:23).

Through the Holy Spirit's power, Jesus the Christ continues to reign over his followers. As his body (the church), we exist to serve him. And as individual Christians, our lives are linked to him in every way, especially through our hope of eternal life (see Rom. 6:1–11). We look forward to his return to earth for us.

Think of it this way: Although we live on earth, we are really citizens of another kingdom, the kingdom of heaven, where Jesus is the ruler. Here's how the apostle Paul put it in Philippians 3:20–21: "But our citizenship is in heaven. And we eagerly await a Savior from there, the Lord Jesus Christ, who, by the power that enables him to bring everything under his control, will transform our lowly bodies so that they will be like his glorious body."

Jesus Christ is not a king without a crown. He is Lord of creation, God's Anointed One, and Lord of the church. He is truly Lord of all!

How would you translate the term *lord* into contemporary language? Of the positions or titles that are used in our society, which ones might fit Jesus?

CHRISTIANS ACCEPT CHRIST'S LORDSHIP

On July 12, 2001, the government of Yugoslavia gave Alexander Karadjordjevic the use of two palaces in Belgrade—Stari Dvor, the Old Palace, and Beli Dvor, the White Palace. That event marked the first official recognition of the crown prince of Yugoslavia in more than sixty years. Born in London in 1945, Alexander is the son of Yugoslavia's last king, Peter II, who fled after Nazi Germany overran the country in 1941. After fifty-one years, the king of Yugoslavia had been invited back into his own home.

Other European kings continue to live in exile without official recognition from their home countries. Albania's Leka I was born in 1939 and fled the country with his family three years later. He lives in South Africa. Romania's former King Michael was forced to abdicate his throne in 1947. He lives in Switzerland. Montenegro's Nicolas Petrovic, born in 1944, is heir to the dynasty that ruled that country until the end of World War I. He is an architect living in Paris.

Can you really be a king if you have no kingdom? Does a king need to be crowned, that is, recognized by his people?

Christians do recognize Christ's lordship. We invite him into the palace of our hearts and crown him as King of our lives. That takes place in several practical ways.

We Acknowledge Christ's Lordship

The first step in accepting Jesus' lordship in our lives is to agree that he is, in fact, the Christ. When Jesus was on earth, many people recognized that truth. It wasn't uncommon for Jesus to prompt this realization by asking a question or provoking some comment.

For example, when Jesus visited Mary and Martha's home after the death of their brother, Lazarus, Jesus made some startling statements about himself. Then he asked Martha, "Do you believe this?" Martha said, "Yes, Lord . . . I believe that you are the Messiah, the Son of God, who is to come into the world" (John 11:26–27).

On another occasion, Jesus asked the disciples what others were saying about him. Finally, he asked them directly, "'But what about you? . . . Who do you say I am?' Peter answered, 'You are the Messiah'" (Mark 8:29).

At other times, people realized who Jesus was after they heard his teaching or observed his miracles. Even his death led some to accept his lordship. As he died on the cross, one bystander, a Roman centurion, looked on and said, "Surely this man was the Son of God!" (Mark 15:39).

Do you believe that Jesus is the Christ? What would it take to convince you that he is?

We Surrender Control

When we accept the fact that Jesus is Lord, we concede control of our lives to him. We give up our claim to authority.

Since we like being master of our own lives, we don't surrender easily. Often, surrendering to Christ does not happen at the moment of conversion. Most people who come to Christ for forgiveness give little thought to the future. Burdened by the guilt of sin, they seek the freedom of forgiveness, and rightly so. They confess their sin and acknowledge Christ as their Savior.

Owning Christ as Lord goes deeper than that. It looks to the future and involves consecrating (setting apart) one's entire life to him.

Jesus called his disciples to do that when he said, "Whoever wants to be my disciple must deny themselves and take up their cross and follow me" (Mark 8:34). The apostle Paul testified to that experience when he said, "I have been crucified with Christ and I no longer live, but Christ lives in me" (Gal. 2:20). Those statements reveal a person who has given up all claims to his or her life and is willing to die, even, for the sake of Christ.

Making Christ Lord of our lives requires an act of the will that says, "I give up control of my life to Christ. I lay all of my abilities, resources, and plans at his feet. I own him as my master."

It's tempting to believe that we might share control of our lives with Christ. We certainly want forgiveness from sin and a good relationship with God, but is it really necessary to give *all* of our life to Christ?

In a word, yes.

Jesus offered simple wisdom with profound meaning when he said, "No one can serve two masters" (Matt. 6:24). Using money as a specific example, he made the point that it's impossible to live for long with divided loyalty. You can't please two bosses. Competing demands eventually will drive a person to serve God or self—never both. Jesus must have first place in our lives, or—as a purely practical matter—he will have none at all.

Have you consecrated your life to Christ? If so, what led you to make that choice? If not, what is the main obstacle to your surrender?

We Live a New Life

Some milestones in life mark dramatic turning points. When you start school, get married, have a baby, or retire, for example, your life changes dramatically.

Accepting Christ as Lord is like that. Our lives are not the same as they were before. Paul explained that our new life in Christ is just that: a new life. We begin to think and act differently. "Therefore, if anyone is in Christ, the new creation has come: The old has gone, the new is here!" (2 Cor. 5:17).

Jesus said, "Anyone who loves me will obey my teaching. . . . Anyone who does not love me will not obey my teaching" (John 14:23–24). That's pretty clear. If Christ truly is our Lord, we will give him authority in our lives. We'll listen to what he says and obey his commands.

So as Christians, we demonstrate that Jesus is our Lord by thinking and behaving in changed ways. We will make it a point to know Jesus' character and to imitate it in our lives.

That change both subtracts from our lives and adds to them. On one hand, there are some things that we will avoid. The Bible refers to this as putting off the *old self*. On the other hand, there are new thoughts and behaviors that we'll acquire. The Bible refers to this change as putting on the *new self*. Paul described that process in Ephesians 4:22–24: "You were taught, with regard to your former way of life, to put off your old self, which is being corrupted by its deceitful desires; to be made new in the attitude of your minds; and to put on the new self, created to be like God in true righteousness and holiness."

The apostle Peter shared some practical ways of doing that. He implored us to "make every effort to add to your faith goodness; and to goodness, knowledge; and to knowledge, self-control; and to self-control, perseverance; and to perseverance, godliness; and to godliness, mutual affection; and to mutual affection, love" (2 Pet. 1:5–7). Owning Christ as Lord involves making daily choices that build on the foundation of virtue in our lives. We choose to think and act differently because of our allegiance to Jesus Christ.

The Old Self: Acts of the Sinful Nature Galatians 5:19–21	**The New Self: Fruit of the Spirit Galatians 5:22–23**
Sexual immorality	Love
Impurity and debauchery	Joy
Idolatry and witchcraft	Peace
Hatred	Forbearance (patience)
Discord and jealousy	Kindness
Fits of rage	Goodness
Selfish ambition	Faithfulness
Dissensions and factions	Gentleness
Drunkenness and orgies	Self-control

Putting off the old self involves changing our minds. Paul wrote, "Clothe yourselves with the Lord Jesus Christ, and do not think about how to gratify the desires of the flesh" (Rom. 13:14). We must begin to weave Jesus Christ's attitudes and teachings into our lives and not allow our minds to dwell on the old ways. That's a process that may take some time.

How is that process going in your life? The following questions may help diagnose the state of your spiritual growth:

- Do I make an effort to know Christ's teaching and obey it?
- Is the old self still in control of some areas of my life?
- Do I ever deliberately ignore God's will in my life?
- Do I think more about what Jesus would do or more about what I want in a given situation?
- Can I see growth in my life since I acknowledged Christ as Lord?
- Do others see changes as a result of Christ's presence in my life?

What is the next change you need to make in putting off the old self and being obedient to Jesus Christ?

We Trust Him

Have you ever been a passenger in your own car? When someone else is at the wheel, it's hard to keep from offering advice. While it's helpful to rotate drivers on a long trip, we typically try to get back behind the wheel as quickly as possible. That's especially true if there's heavy traffic, rain, snow, or some other hazard present.

We often do the same thing when it comes to the lordship of Christ. We give him control for a while, but when life becomes challenging or painful, we get back behind the wheel.

That's what Peter did when he walked on water to meet Jesus (see Matt. 14:22–32). At first, Peter trusted Jesus and walked toward him with no problems. But when he saw the wind and the waves, he began to sink.

We often do the same. We yield to Christ's lordship when things are going well. But when we face job stress, marital trouble, illness, or unhappiness, we forget about Christ and make decisions for ourselves.

Owning Christ as Lord means that we trust him—all the time.

Jesus taught us to trust God for everything from the food we eat to the clothes we wear. God knows our needs and has promised to take care of us (see Matt. 6:25–32). Jesus also promised that he would not desert us (see Matt. 28:20; John 14:18) and would send us the counselor or advocate, the Holy Spirit, to accompany us (see John 14:16). When Christ is Lord, we have more security—not less—because he's able to provide for us.

Do you tend to take back control of your life from Christ? What situations cause you to doubt?

CHRIST'S LORDSHIP BRINGS CONTENTMENT

Imagine you visit a restaurant where the dining room is dirty, the service is slow, and the food is lousy. Several months later, you see a sign at the restaurant that reads "Under New Management." You visit again and find that things have changed. The dining room is sparkling clean, the service is prompt, and you have a delightful meal. New management makes a difference.

That's true in life too. When we surrender our lives to Christ, the "new manager" will make changes for the better. When we surrender control of our lives to Christ, there are good results.

We Have Peace

Peace is a rare commodity in this world. Nations, neighborhoods, workplaces, homes—just about any place people are together—there will probably be a fight.

The reason people can't get along with each other is that they don't have peace with themselves or with God. Since the beginning, our sin has separated us from God and caused trouble in our personal relationships (see Gen. 3:1–24).

But Jesus brings peace. He said, "Peace I leave with you; my peace I give you" (John 14:27). When he controls our lives, we'll be at peace.

That's possible because he made peace with God for us. Paul wrote, "Since we have been justified through faith, we have peace with God through our Lord Jesus Christ" (Rom. 5:1). Jesus' death atoned for our sin, which made that peace with God for us. "For God was pleased to have all his fullness dwell in him, and through him to reconcile to himself all things, whether things on earth or things in heaven, by making peace through his blood, shed on the cross" (Col. 1:19–20). That means that we're not at odds with God anymore. We have peace with him, so we can be at peace with ourselves and with others.

In what ways does your attitude about yourself affect your relationships with others?

We Have Power

When Christ controls your life, you're never truly on your own. You have God's power at your disposal.

When Jesus went to heaven, he sent the Holy Spirit to his disciples. Through the power of the Spirit, they were enabled to speak the word of God boldly and perform many miracles. (See the book of Acts, especially chapter 2.)

That same Holy Spirit is available to all believers in Christ today. The Holy Spirit gives us abilities, or gifts, that we wouldn't otherwise have (see Rom. 12:3–8; 1 Cor. 12:12–31; Eph. 4:10–13).

Although the apostle Paul faced many difficult circumstances in life, including shipwreck, poverty, and imprisonment, he said, "I can do all this through [Christ] who gives me strength" (Phil. 4:13). When Jesus is Lord, we have the confidence and God-given ability to face the most challenging circumstances.

What are you facing right now, or what challenging thing has God called you to do?

We Have Victory

It's ironic. Most of the time, we work very hard at maintaining control of our lives, yet we almost never succeed. In spite of what we'd like to think, we're not very good at controlling our circumstances, or even our own behavior! How often, for instance, have you said, "I wish I hadn't done that" or "When will I learn to control my temper?"

We probably fail more often than we succeed at managing our lives. The apostle Paul called that experience being a "slave to sin" (Rom. 7:14). Without Christ, we're not really in control, even of our own choices.

With Christ in charge, that changes. Through the power of the Holy Spirit living within us, we have freedom from sin and are able to become the people we really want to be. Paul wrote, "Through Christ Jesus the law of the Spirit who gives life has set you free from the law of sin and death" (Rom. 8:2). The Holy Spirit enables us to act on what before were only good intentions.

So in a real sense, we have more freedom when Christ is in control and we're not! That is sometimes called having victory over sin. It's a direct result of accepting Christ's lordship over our lives.

We Have Hope

What happens when you die? Everybody wonders about that, and nearly every religion offers a different view. None of them do much to quell the uneasy feeling we have when forced to think about the end of life.

Jesus Christ is Lord not only of life, but also of death. The Bible teaches that "he is the beginning and the firstborn from among the dead, so that in everything he might have the supremacy" (Col. 1:18).

By rising from the dead, Jesus showed that he conquered it. As Lord of death, he has the power to give life to anyone (see Rom. 6:1–6). That's one of the last messages he gave to his disciples. Shortly before his death, Jesus said, "Do not let your hearts be troubled. You believe in God; believe also in me. My father's house has many rooms; if that were not so, would I have told you that I am going there to prepare a place for you? And if I go and prepare a place for you, I will come back and take you to be with me that you also may be where I am" (John 14:1–3). By trusting in Christ as our Lord and Savior, we gain his promise of eternal life.

As he so often did, the apostle Paul summed up this incredible hope in Philippians 3:20: "But our citizenship is in heaven. And we eagerly await a Savior from there, the Lord Jesus Christ."

A Christian has no need to fear death. Jesus Christ is Lord—in death and life.

WHICH DO YOU CHOOSE?

When you give your life to Christ, you do not lose your autonomy; you gain his authority, power, and help. The result is not slavery, but freedom to enjoy life for the first time.

When we try to control our own lives, the results can be frustrating. We lack peace. We fear death. We carry a world of problems all by ourselves. When Jesus is Lord, we have peace. The power of God is available to us. We are released from guilt and fear.

Which do you choose? Who is the lord of your life?

WEEK 2

SUBMIT YOUR WILL TO GOD'S

Therefore, I urge you, brothers and sisters, in view of God's mercy, to offer your bodies as a living sacrifice, holy and pleasing to God—this is your true and proper worship. Do not conform to the pattern of this world, but be transformed by the renewing of your mind. Then you will be able to test and approve what God's will is—his good, pleasing and perfect will.

—Romans 12:1–2

BIBLE BASICS

- Romans 12:1–2
- Colossians 4:12

Do you know God's will for your life? How would you find out according to Romans 12:1–2?

A PLAN FOR YOUR LIFE

Have you ever heard someone say, "God has a plan for your life"? You might have responded with a bit of sarcasm, saying, "Yeah, sure!"

Or perhaps the idea that the almighty God has thought specifically about you intrigued you.

The term *God's will* is used so freely that most people pay it little attention. Can it be true that God has a plan for your life? And if he does, how can you know what it is?

As a beginning point, let's understand that God has a general will for all people. There are some things that he desires for every human being. Beyond that, you can learn to discover his specific will for you.

Let's find out how.

KNOWING GOD'S GENERAL WILL

Understanding God's plan for your life begins with some basics. There are some things God desires for all people. When you understand these, you'll be on your way to discovering God's plan for your entire life.

Salvation

The first and most important element of God's plan for your life is salvation. The Bible declares that God does not want "anyone to perish, but everyone to come to repentance" (2 Pet. 3:9). How did you come to repentance and faith in Jesus as your Savior?

Holiness

Not only does God want everyone to be saved from the penalty for sin, he also wants all Christians to be saved from the power of sin so that they can live in a way that glorifies him (see 1 Cor. 10:31). God wants you to do more than simply ask to be forgiven for past sins. He wants to break sin's power in your life.

It is important for every believer to understand that growing Christians should glorify God in everything they do. Whether going to school, working, playing, shopping, interacting in the family, serving in the community, or whatever it might be, Christians are to live every day for God's glory.

Service

The apostle Peter wrote to a group of Christians, identifying them as "chosen" to be a "royal priesthood" of people who were to declare God's praises (1 Pet. 2:5, 9). From this we learn that God wants all believers to serve him in whatever we do and tell people about Christ and his great love.

It is God's will for every one of us to be a priest who gives him glory, regardless of the profession we choose.

List three people who are not in vocational Christian ministry but are everyday "priests" of God.

FINDING GOD'S SPECIFIC WILL

Once we understand the basics of God's plan for our lives, we can move on to discover his specific will for our lives. One day, Jesus taught his disciples to pray. He used a model prayer that included a plea for God's will to be done here on earth (see Matt. 6:10).

Since Jesus told us to pray that God's will be done, it is fair to believe that God does have a specific will for each us. The big question we each must ask is, "How can I know God's plan for my life? Beyond God's general will revealed in Scripture, how can I be sure of God's specific will for my life?"

Most maturing Christians would say that God uses clear principles and patterns when communicating with people. If his Word, the Bible, is silent about some specific issue, we may follow proven biblical principles and patterns as a guide. What follows are eight questions that reveal principles for discerning God's specific will. Your answers to these questions will probably point you in the right direction.

Am I Fully Surrendered to God?

The first question concerns your commitment to knowing God and doing his will. Are you fully surrendered to God? Have you acknowledged Jesus Christ as Lord of your life, and are you willing to do whatever he wants you to do (see Luke 9:23; Gal. 2:20)? Divine leadership comes from divine presence, so if you have not fully surrendered yourself to God and are not enjoying his active presence in your life, you probably won't be able to discern his will. The Holy Spirit brings God's presence into every believer's life. God's Holy Spirit will guide you into all truth if you are fully surrendered to him (see John 14:15, 17, 25–26; 16:12–15).

Have I Studied the Bible?

If you want to know God, a good place to start is with his Word, the Bible. Have you studied the Bible in order to become acquainted with God? What principles, commands, or prohibitions do you see in Scripture that might guide you in your search for God's will (see Ps. 119:105, 130)? Have you discovered any promises or motivating verses on the subject? If you believe you know God's will for your life, do you see affirmation in God's Word? Study the Bible to help you understand God's will. And be fair in your use of Scripture. Don't pick out only those verses that seem to support your own desires. Let God's Word speak for itself.

Have I Prayed about It?

Many individuals do everything to discover God's will except ask him. They listen to preachers, read books, and seek inspiration from a variety of sources, but they fail to get alone with God and ask him. The Bible is filled with stories of people who asked God for specific answers and received them. If you want to know God's will for your life, ask him (see Phil. 4:6).

When you pray, take time to be quiet and listen for God's answer. Shut off the television, radio, computer, and every other device and spend some time with God. Try it for even a brief period of time. Talk to God, and then listen for his voice.

You may be wondering, "How will I know if it's God's voice that I'm hearing?" Martin Wells Knapp wrote a wonderful book in 1892 to answer that question. Knapp indicated four key elements for testing our impressions to see if they are the voice of God.

Does It Match Biblical Truth? First, is the impression in agreement with Scripture, or does it contradict Scripture? God's leadership always matches biblical truth. That's why it's important for every believer to know the Bible. If you do not know the Bible, then you have no yardstick for telling whether your impressions measure up against God's known will.

Is It the Right Thing to Do? Knapp wrote, "Impressions which are from God are always right. They may be contrary to our feelings, our prejudices and our natural inclinations, but they are always right."[1] Some of what we need to consider is simple common sense. Does this promote God and godly principles, or is it selfish or worldly?

Are There Providential Circumstances That Support This Impression? When God is leading, he goes before us and opens doors that make possible what seems impossible. If your impression is truly

God's will, you can expect opportunities to arise that will enable you to proceed with it. Does it appear that God is working to bring about what you feel called to do?

Is It a Reasonable Thing to Do? What is reasonable is sometimes hard to define. When a young woman tells her parents that God has called her to be a missionary in some foreign country, her parents may not think it is reasonable. However, one might look past the emotional response of loving parents to ask, "Has God ever called others to do something similar? Has it succeeded?" Ask yourself and others, "Does my impression sound reasonable?"

Does It Match My God-Given Gifts and Abilities?

If you can't throw a baseball more than twenty feet but you think God may want you to pitch for the New York Yankees, it's safe to say that you are not in tune with God's will. However, if you find that friends constantly ask your advice about their difficulties and you find great fulfillment in encouraging them, your experience and abilities would confirm that your growing desire to be a counselor is God's will for your life. God has uniquely gifted each of us, and he did it so we could find fulfillment in using our abilities to serve him (see 1 Cor. 12:4–6).

Does the Holy Spirit Continually Bring This to Mind?

When you pray and visit with other Christians, do you seem continually drawn toward a particular issue, or does your impression seem to grow weaker with time? If what you desire to do is from God, his Holy Spirit will constantly bring your mind back to it. You will have a growing conviction that it is something you must do.

What Is the Advice of Mature Christians on This Issue?

Mature Christians who have experienced God's leadership for many years are a wonderful resource for sorting through the myriad options before you and helping you find God's specific will. The Bible tells us to listen to and accept advice because it will make us wise (see Prov. 19:20).

Do I Have Peace about This Issue?

A sense of peace generally accompanies the will of God. Do you have inner peace about the issue as you pray and accept counsel from wise Christians? Or does the discussion of this issue create a spirit of turmoil for you (see Col. 3:15; Phil. 4:6–7)? Something may be good and godly but simply not the right thing for you. When you arrive at God's will, you will have peace.

Is This the Right Time?

God is perfect and his timing is always perfect too. Ask yourself whether you are pushing the issue under your own time schedule or trusting God to work in his own time. Or are you holding back too long before stepping out? If you are moving on God's schedule, things will tend to fall into place (see Ps. 27:14; Lam. 3:26; 2 Cor. 8:11).

If you are trying to discover God's will for your life, you may want to write down these questions in a journal and ponder them in God's presence. After a time of personal worship, consider each question, asking God to speak to you. If the issue at hand is an emotional one, give greater weight to the more objective questions—those that don't rely heavily on personal feelings or opinions.

FREQUENTLY ASKED QUESTIONS ABOUT GOD'S WILL

Discerning God's will is not a black-and-white issue. Few subjects raise more questions in a growing believer's mind. Yet it is possible to know God and to sense his personal will. The responses to these common questions may help you to understand the process of discerning God's will.

Does God Ever Reveal His Will by Spectacular Means?

Yes. The Bible shows us that God has revealed his will through some amazing methods. The story of Paul's conversion is one example (see Acts 9). The apostle Peter's incredible vision is another (see Acts 10). Today, many Christians report spectacular revelations of God's will.

It's important to note, however, that these are exceptional happenings. God usually doesn't reveal himself in extraordinary ways. If God knows that we need miraculous guidance, he will surely give it. Yet it's best to concentrate our attention on learning to discern and discover his will through more common, usual means.

Are People Really Called to Full-Time Christian Ministry?

Yes. Not every Christian is called to vocational Christian service—that is, to work as a pastor or missionary, or in some other Christian vocation. Yet, God does call some people to serve him as a full-time job. People around us will not come to know Jesus unless some of us are willing to go and tell them in this way (see Rom. 10:12–15).

Marks of a Calling. If you are wondering whether or not you are called to vocational ministry, some basic principles may help guide your decision. John Wesley identified three "marks" that are evident in a person whom God calls to vocational ministry.

The first is *grace*. Is the person converted? Does he or she display the fruit of the Spirit by living a holy life? The second mark is *gifts*. This refers to the gifts of the Spirit. Does the person have the ability to understand, reason, speak, communicate, and provide loving care and leadership. *Fruit* is the third mark. This refers to the person's effectiveness in ministry. Do people come to know Christ and grow as a result of this person's influence?

When these three marks are evident, the person will likely also have an abiding sense of a divine call that will motivate him or her to full-time Christian vocational service.

Assessing Your Call. If you feel that you may be called to the ministry, look at these areas of your life to help confirm that calling. First, examine your gifts. If God is calling you to full-time Christian service, he will put within you the spiritual gifts and natural talents that support such a calling. Do your gifts and talents complement what you believe God is asking you to do?

Many people do not know what their spiritual gifts are. Therefore it's difficult to assess what they may be called to do. If you are unsure of your spiritual gifts, seek your pastor's advice. You may also wish to complete a spiritual gifts assessment inventory. If you are called to ministry, your spiritual gifts will support and complement that vocation. (See Rom. 12:6–8; 1 Cor. 12:8–11, 28–31; and Eph. 4:11–12 for more information on spiritual gifts.)

Second, if you are called to ministry, it's likely that mature Christians around you will affirm that impression. Do other Christians ask you to share your testimony because when you do something good often seems to happen? Do other Christians pursue you for counsel because you seem to have a keen insight into God's Word? God nearly always uses spiritually mature Christians to affirm the call.

The third area to examine when assessing your call to ministry is your personal interest. Is this something you want to do? Do you enjoy and find fulfillment in helping others discover the truth about God? Do you delight in studying the Bible? Do you find fulfillment in helping others? Your calling will likely relate directly to the things that you enjoy and find fulfilling.

What factors lead you to believe that you are called or are not called to vocational Christian ministry?

Can I Miss God's Will for My Life?

Unfortunately, the answer is yes. God's will begins with salvation, and a person may reject God's gracious offer of forgiveness. Beyond that, God's will includes living every day to his glory. Some people, even Christians, focus more on themselves than on God.

In the same way, it's possible to miss God's specific will for our lives. People like King Saul and Jonah exemplify this. Their disobedience caused them either to stray away from God's will or to miss it entirely. Disobedience will affect us in the same way. Any one of us may miss God's will if we begin to tolerate sin in our lives.

It's important to note that people generally do not miss God's will because they don't know what it is. They miss God's will because they choose not to obey it. This is possible because we have a will of our own. We have the freedom to make choices—God made us that way. As we use that freedom to respond to the Holy Spirit's leading, we are able to bring great glory to God. However, if personal, selfish desires sway us, we may choose to do something other than God's will.

Obedience, therefore, is the most important factor for staying in tune with God's will, and obedience takes place one step at a time. Step-by-step, we *can* walk in God's will.

Do you believe that you have discovered God's will for your life? If not, what will you do to find it?

NOTE

1. Martin Wells Knapp, *Impressions* (Cincinnati, OH: Revivalist Publishing, 1892), 55.

WEEK 3

PREPARE YOUR SOUL FOR BATTLE

For our struggle is not against flesh and blood, but against the rulers, against the authorities, against the powers of this dark world and against the spiritual forces of evil in the heavenly realms.

—Ephesians 6:12

BIBLE BASICS

- Ephesians 6:10–18

Who are the rulers, authorities, and other powers in your life? Where are your spiritual battles to be fought?

THE REALITY OF SPIRITUAL WARFARE

Spiritual warfare is real. Spiritual battles are fought not only in heaven and hell, but also in the hearts and minds of human beings. Spiritual contests take place wherever souls are at stake.

There are perhaps two dangers in dealing with the subject of spiritual warfare. One is that the reality of evil might be minimized—that we might deny the existence of such things as witchcraft, demonic possession, or the occult. But such things are real, and we must take them seriously. The other danger, however, is that we might become overly concerned with those matters and ignore the spiritual battles that take place in our own minds and homes every day.

The latter is probably the greater danger. Since activities such as witchcraft or the occult are clearly evil, the simple way to deal with them is to avoid them. It's in other areas that Satan is likely to direct his forces. The Bible suggests that he is often indirect, subtle, and devious in his assaults and even "masquerades as an angel of light" (2 Cor. 11:14). Consequently, we will fight our spiritual battles in ourselves, our homes, our communities, our churches—indeed, wherever good people are found.

Yes, we should be concerned about satanic cults, witchcraft, and similar evils. These typically become battlefields for people who have been led into them gradually as they dabbled with such things as Ouija boards or astrology. Some Christians are enamored by the weird, the spectacular, or the occult, and treat them as entertainment. As a result, they gradually accept things that are contrary to the faith. Believers in Christ should have nothing to do with overt evil. As the Bible says, "God is light; in him there is no darkness at all" (1 John 1:5).

The primary spiritual battle that you face is the battle within you—the battle for the self.

SPIRITUAL SELF-DEFENSE

Since we are eternal creatures only in the spiritual sense, it is interesting that so many people pay little attention to anything but the temporary features of themselves—the body and the mind. It's easy to become so focused on our mental, emotional, and physical lives that that we give little or no attention to our spiritual selves. That leaves us ill prepared to cope with the inevitable battle for the spiritual self. Many of us don't even recognize that there is a war going on.

The renowned psychiatrist Sigmund Freud believed that the two most important issues in human behavior were the aggressive instinct and sex. Other psychologists believe that altruistic tendencies are most important in explaining our behavior. Still others see human beings as basically depraved; and yet others, including B. F. Skinner, have seen human beings as blank slates on which experience will write.

All of those explanations of human nature overlook spirituality. As Christians we know that we are primarily and eternally spiritual creatures. We are complex physical, mental, and emotional beings, yet we are primarily spiritual. Therefore, our spiritual development and care are most important.

Of course it is imperative that we attend to all of our needs. We must develop and care for our minds and our bodies. Careful preparation in spirit, mind, and body will arm us for the battles that have eternal consequences. We must pay attention to the mind-body-spirit interaction if we are to triumph in spiritual warfare.

Spiritual Care

Conflict among the physical, emotional, intellectual, and spiritual selves is common. The apostle Paul referred to this inner warfare when he wrote, "So I find this law at work: Although I want to do good, evil is right there with me. For in my inner being I delight in God's law; but I see another law at work in me, waging war against the law of my mind and making me a prisoner of the law of sin at work within me" (Rom. 7:21–23).

In this passage, Paul described the continual battle within that he could not win in his own strength. However, he later described how he could obtain victory through the power of Christ living in him. The resources for this inner spiritual conflict and for spiritual warfare in a hostile world are identical. These battles are won "'not by might nor by power, but by my Spirit,' says the LORD Almighty" (Zech. 4:6).

Paul identified the "armor" for this spiritual battle in Ephesians, chapter 6. The shoes are *readiness*. The shield is *faith*. The helmet is *salvation*. The body armor is *righteousness*. And the offensive weapon, the sword of the Spirit, is the *Word of God*.

Knowing that we face spiritual battles, we must arm ourselves by actively strengthening our spiritual selves and becoming well versed in the Scriptures. Daily equipping is essential. Reading God's Word, communing with him in prayer and meditation, and affiliating with others who are committed to the spiritual disciplines are essential ways to deal with spiritual conflict.

What are you doing to arm yourself for spiritual battle?

USES OF SPIRITUAL ARMOR

	Self	Home	Community	Church
Belt of Truth	Personal intergrity	Valuing others	Public integrity	Intolerance of false teaching
Breastplate of Righteousness	Good intentions	Treating everyone fairly	Social justice	Inclusiveness
Shoes of the Gospel of Peace	Composure	Willingness to settle disputes	Community involvement	Compassion ministry
Shield of Faith	Consistent belief	Family worship	Faith-based decision making	Truth valued over personal comfort
Helmet of Salvation	Assurance of relationship with God	Witnessing to children	Sharing the faith with others	Evangelistic ministry
Sword of Truth (God's Word)	Knowledge	Teaching children about the faith	Biblically authentic lifestyle	Consistent Bible teaching

Physical Care

This is not to say that Christians should focus on spiritual issues to the neglect of others. We must also deal with psychological and physical issues if we are to be at our best spiritually. Some individuals are defeated spiritually as a consequence of neglecting their physical and psychological well-being. Perhaps you have heard of some folks who reject medical care in the name of spirituality. They believe that accepting medical intervention for physical problems amounts to a denial of faith. While we know that God can heal miraculously, we also believe that he intends for us to do what we can—including using medical science—to care for our own bodies.

Neglect of our physical needs is poor preparation for spiritual warfare. It's important to eat properly, rest, and preserve our physical health as best we can. Physical health is an advantage in spiritual combat.

Psychological Care

We must also attend to our psychological selves. The lines between physical and psychological issues are sometimes ill-defined. For example, the need for regular, adequate, quality sleep is absolutely essential to good psychological function. Many experts believe that sleep deficiencies underlie an array of mental and physical problems that represent the major preventable health issues in our world today. It is interesting that so many people worry about poor sleep only when it interferes with other routines, as in the case of insomnia. The number one problem in this area is that people simply don't *regularly* allot themselves their needed amount of sleep, thereby accumulating a sleep debt that can have devastating consequences physically, psychologically, and spiritually.

Proper care to all our needs is essential if we are to triumph spiritually. Depressed Christians are always prime targets for the Enemy of their spiritual selves, and we know that people are more likely to be depressed if they neglect their physical and psychological health.

What is the current state of your physical and emotional health? In what ways might that affect your spiritual well-being?

SPIRITUAL BATTLEGROUNDS

To be sure, not all spiritual battles are inner conflicts. There are outside forces that will attempt to destroy us. These need not be spectacular. The Enemy of our eternal souls will use the most ordinary, mundane things to defeat us spiritually. People, places, and things may all be turned to Satan's advantage. There is no such thing as being so spiritual as to escape the efforts of the dark forces of evil to overthrow us. Think about Job. This most righteous man of his time became the target of the Devil. His life became a battleground for a cosmic struggle between good and evil.

Jesus said that we are to be the salt in society. He pointed to the reality that the world is a hostile place and that we must penetrate it for good. When we do that, we engage in spiritual warfare, taking Christ's redeeming presence into all the places we go. By affirming Christian values, practicing a Christian lifestyle, and showing Christ's love to others in every place we inhabit, we engage the world for God—we do spiritual warfare!

Here are some of the places where you might find yourself engaged in spiritual battle.

The Home

The home may be a battleground in spiritual warfare; and often, the battle there is lost. Even Christian homes sometimes fall prey to the forces of spiritual darkness. Adultery, the abuse or neglect of children, and divorce are realities even in the Christian community.

One reason for a home's spiritual collapse is the father's surrender of moral authority. In too many cases, a father may be absent during his children's critical developmental years.

Marriage is another point of spiritual conflict. Given the prevailing attitude toward marital fidelity in our culture, Christian spouses must spend extra effort building and preserving strong marriages. By undermining a marriage, Satan affects many people—the couple, their children, and extended family members. Building a strong marriage is a defense in the battle for the home.

Entertainment

Entertainment is another point of spiritual conflict. Television, movies, popular music, magazines, movies, video games, the Internet—the number of entertainment sources that are available to us is staggering. Unfortunately, Satan has turned many of these to his advantage, bombarding our children and us with ungodly messages and temptation.

No form of communication is evil in itself, yet Christians must be savvy in their use of the entertainment media. Here are some questions to consider when choosing entertainment:

- What is the underlying message? Does it reinforce my spiritual disciplines or undermine them?
- How much time will I spend doing this? Is it a wise use of my time?
- Are there alternatives that would better support my desire to keep a pure mind, heart, and body?
- What place does entertainment have in my life? Is that appropriate?

Peer pressure among children and teenagers is perhaps stronger today than ever. Parents often fear their children will view them negatively if they censor certain kinds of entertainment. Yet, isn't it reasonable to assume that our spiritual enemies will take advantage of this battlefield? It is better to risk our children's wrath than to lose them. We must use entertainment wisely if we are to remain spiritually fit.

About how many hours a week do you spend using various entertainment media? Do you think your use of entertainment is balanced? If not, what changes will you make?

Substance Abuse

Drugs—legal and illegal—and alcohol are a part of everyday life in North America. Each of us probably knows someone whose life has been ruined by abuse of these substances. For the most part, we are exposed to these temptations in the community, not at church. Some Christians, however, seem to minimize the danger of substance abuse by modeling behaviors that set a poor example.

Nicotine addiction is now considered a psychiatric disorder, listed in the same sections of a mental health diagnostic manual as marijuana and cocaine. Many believe that beer is a relatively benign beverage, yet it is the drink of choice for many alcoholics. We are perhaps so concerned about dramatic new problems that we have overlooked some of the old ones—things that Satan still uses to ensnare people.

Avoidance of harmful substances continues to be the only sure way to have spiritual victory over them. Proponents of the lottery have been known to say, "You can't win if you don't play." When it comes to addictive substances, you can't lose if you don't use.

Do any of your lifestyle habits represent a danger to your spiritual life? If so, what will you do about them?

Wealth and Possessions

It's tempting to be caught up in the "must have" mentality of our world. Satan uses that way of thinking as a trap to distract us from the things that really matter. Jesus once told of a wealthy man who became engrossed in the search to "have it all." As soon as he filled one barn with goods, he planned to tear it down and build a bigger one. Bigger, more, better, faster. His philosophy of life was similar to the consumer mind-set that tempts us. In the story, God confronted the man, and said, "You fool! This very night your life will be demanded from you. Then who will get what you have prepared for yourself?" (Luke 12:20).

Satan wants to keep our attention on ourselves. Tempting us with the desire for wealth and possessions is an effective way to do that. Being spiritually fit means taking God's view of things—seeing them as tools to accomplish a purpose, not as trinkets that bring satisfaction.

Is your view of material things in line with God's? These questions may help you decide:

- Do I spend more time with material things or with people?
- Am I more concerned about my retirement account or my relationship with God?
- How often do I say, "I've *got* to have that"?
- How many things do I have that I know I don't need?

The Occult

Rationalism is the dominant philosophy of this scientific age, and it often leaves no space for spiritual concerns. Is it any wonder that false religions attract so many people? Rationalism doesn't meet their needs for real meaning in life.

Many claim to be rationalists, perhaps even naturalists, who are fascinated by stories of ghosts, demon possession, devils, and witches. In the days when people accepted the spirit world without much question, we may have been better prepared to deal with such things. Now that we are accustomed to seeing a cause-and-effect explanation for everything in life, we may be more vulnerable to attacks from the dark world.

Christians must be aware of the occult and be on guard against it. We have no cause for alarm because Jesus Christ is Lord over all the world, including demonic forces. Yet dark forces do have power in the world, and can ensnare the unwary. That's why believers in Christ avoid witchcraft in all of its forms (see Gal. 5:20). Even things that seem harmless, such as Ouija boards, tarot cards, fantasy role-playing, and astrology can be dangerous. They can open the door to contact with the demonic world.

Worship

From time to time, people get caught up in all sorts of marginal activities in the name of worship. People have done the most bizarre things, including snake handling, drinking poison, and handling fire because they believe such activities are authentic expressions of Christian worship.

And then some believe that truly spiritual worship always involves some sort of highly charged emotional activity. Emotion, of course, is an element in most spiritual experiences. In those cases, however, emotion is the effect of spirituality, not the cause.

We're not likely to see snake handling in church these days, but emotional arousal often substitutes for genuine worship. In that way, emotional experience becomes an end in itself. The danger in that is that people are much more vulnerable to the power of suggestion when they are emotionally aroused. The forces of evil can take advantage of those who are in a state of near emotional frenzy.

The Cult of Celebrity

Our culture loves celebrities. Interestingly, when people are well-known, we become fascinated by their opinions about nearly everything. We want to know what breakfast cereal a star athlete eats, and we avidly listen to relationship advice given by movie stars. Celebrities influence everything from our clothing styles to our political opinions.

Yet many celebrities are nonbelievers and may hold unchristian—even anti-Christian—views on matters of faith and family. Too often, celebrities model a lifestyle that glorifies self-adulation and self-indulgence.

To remain spiritually fit, we must choose Christian role models. Carefully evaluate the lifestyle and message of those whom you honor with your respect and attention.

Who are your role models? Why do you choose to model yourself after them?

TAKING THE OFFENSIVE

Our spiritual warfare is not to be just defensive. Remember the old sports adage, "The best defense is a good offense!" We put on the whole armor of God not just to protect ourselves, but to destroy evil as well. Christians are to be salt and light (see Matt. 5:13–16), penetrating the darkness in our communities and engaging evil where we find it. Sometimes we're timid about doing that.

Many believers *are* active in penetrating the darkness around them. Compassion is our motivation for offensive spiritual warfare. Having been freed from the power of darkness, we want to free others as well. Evangelism, social activism, and even political lobbying are ways we can change our communities for the better. In the matter of spiritual warfare, there can be no pacifists. Doing nothing for God in the world amounts to a victory for the Enemy. As believers in Jesus Christ, we really are "Christian soldiers," armed with God's Word, protected by his Spirit, and ready for a fight!

What is the most obvious manifestation of evil in your community? What might you do to fight against it?

WEEK 4

FORTIFY YOUR HEART TO SUFFER

But those who suffer he delivers in their suffering;
he speaks to them in their affliction.

—Job 36:15

BIBLE BASICS

- 2 Corinthians 1:3–7
- 1 Peter 4:12–16

Based on these Scriptures, would you say that suffering is a good thing or a bad thing? Why?

THE REALITY OF SUFFERING

Several years ago, Dr. Paul Brand, a longtime medical missionary to India and pioneer in the treatment of leprosy, published a book entitled

Pain, the Gift Nobody Wants. Dr. Brand's interesting view of pain resulted from his research into leprosy, a disease that often results in the absence of feeling in various parts of the patient's body. This absence of feeling, or anesthesia, frequently resulted in complications that were difficult to treat. Ordinarily, we think of freedom from pain as a blessing, and we search for ways to alleviate the discomfort of suffering. In fact, pain can be valuable since it indicates the presence of a disease or injury. God allows our suffering, even though we would rather he didn't!

Suffering in any form attracts our attention quickly and causes us to seek relief. Generally, it indicates a problem in one of three areas: body, spirit, or mind.

Physical	Spiritual	Emotional
Illness	Sin	Abuse
Injury	Guilt	Rejection
Hunger	Unforgiveness	Depression
Persecution	Separation from God	Regret

Physical suffering may result from illness, injury, or hunger. Or it may result from factors outside the self, such as neglect, abuse, or persecution. When we identify a physical source for suffering, we seek medical treatment. Too often, there is no easy solution to a physical problem and the sufferer must endure pain.

Spiritual suffering results from sin and the guilt it produces. This may be a more frequent cause of discomfort, even physical discomfort, than we choose to admit. We read in 1 Corinthians 6:19–20: "Do you not know that your bodies are temples of the Holy Spirit, who is in you, whom you have received from God? You are not your own; you were bought at a price. Therefore, honor God with your bodies." Pain produced by spiritual trauma has no medical cure. It needs a spiritual solution.

Some suffering has an emotional cause. The trauma experienced, for example, by an abused child is impossible to measure. Physical or relational distress can produce emotional suffering that continues even after the source of pain is removed. Those who have experienced this type of suffering have found that the promises of God's Word can provide healing.

In each of these cases, a ready cure for suffering may be available. Medical treatment may alleviate physical suffering. Confession, repentance, and forgiveness cure spiritual suffering. Medical and psychological treatments often can relieve emotional distress.

But there are times when suffering cannot be relieved; it must be endured. What then?

Which cause of suffering—physical, spiritual, or emotional—is the most difficult for you to deal with? Why?

BIBLICAL EXAMPLES OF SUFFERING

When we think of suffering, the biblical character Job immediately comes to mind. It would be hard to name anyone, except Christ himself, who suffered more than Job. Yet, when even his own wife advised him to curse God and die, Job replied, "You are talking like a foolish woman. Shall we accept good from God, and not trouble?" (Job 2:10). Job's reply shows that it's possible to endure suffering with God's help.

David recognized that "the LORD is a refuge for the oppressed, a stronghold in times of trouble" (Ps. 9:9) and that "in the day of trouble he will keep me safe in his dwelling; he will hide me in the shelter of his sacred tent and set me high upon a rock" (Ps. 27:5).

Jesus himself is our ultimate example of suffering. It's difficult to imagine the terrible physical, mental, and spiritual anguish he endured on the cross. Yet, he endured that pain for our salvation. He was able to face the gravest moment of suffering—death—in triumph.

Scripture shows us that suffering is a reality and that we can endure it through faith in God.

What purpose is there in this pain? Why do we suffer? Conventional wisdom proposes that good things happen to good people while the bad things are reserved for bad people. As you survey your list of family members, friends, and acquaintances, you quickly discover that conventional wisdom in this instance is not entirely right. The apostle Peter wrote, "Dear friends, do not be surprised at the fiery ordeal that has come on you to test you, as though something strange were happening to you. But rejoice inasmuch as you participate in the sufferings of Christ, so that you may be overjoyed when his glory is revealed" (1 Pet. 4:12–13).

To the Christian, the experience of suffering is meaningful. In fact, God chose suffering as the instrument for our redemption. Consider Paul's writing to the Colossians about Christ and his work: "For God was pleased to have all his fullness dwell in him, and through him to reconcile to himself all things, whether things on earth or things in heaven, by making peace through his blood, shed on the cross. Once you were alienated from God and were enemies in your minds because of your evil behavior. But now he has reconciled you by Christ's physical body through death to present you holy in his sight, without blemish and free from accusation" (Col. 1:19–22). Jesus came so that he could suffer and so that we could be reconciled with him. In fact, that was the only way we could be saved!

The apostle Peter went a step further and said that our own suffering plays a role in our Christian development. "Therefore, since Christ suffered in his body, arm yourselves also with the same attitude, because whoever suffers in the body is done with sin" (1 Pet. 4:1). Suffering, then, can be a good thing because it helps to improve our faith. Listen to the apostle James: "Consider it pure joy, my brothers and sisters, whenever you face trials of many kinds, because you know that the testing of your faith produces perseverance. Let perseverance finish its work so that you may be mature and complete, not lacking anything" (James 1:2–4). The writer of Hebrews added, "Endure hardship as discipline; God is treating you as his children. For what children are not disciplined by their father?" (Heb. 12:7).

God allows us to suffer to make us realize our helplessness. He shouts to us in our pain, cutting through our conceit and self-centeredness. When we suffer, our faith increases as we learn to depend upon him.

At times, the link between our suffering and our faith may be obvious. Financial loss, for example, may very quickly cause us to depend upon God and discover that he is faithful to provide. At other times, it may be difficult to see a direct benefit or "happy ending" to every painful situation. As we trust God, however, and grow more mature, we may look back and see that God has been working for our good at all times—even when life seemed to be at its worst. As the apostle Paul promised, "He who began a good work in you will carry it on to completion until the day of Christ Jesus" (Phil. 1:6).

What has caused pain in your life recently? Can you see that God is at work in your suffering? If so, how?

COPING WITH SUFFERING

We cannot control what happens to us. But every one of us can control our response. Your attitude will largely determine how you cope with suffering. As it is in most areas of life, when you suffer, attitude is everything. So how do we face suffering? What follows are five steps for dealing with suffering. For those who suffer, they are stepping-stones to spiritual growth.

Avoid It

Sometimes we suffer because we needlessly endure pain or inflict it upon ourselves. It is obvious advice but still good: Avoid suffering if you can.

God created us wonderfully. Our bodies are a gift from him and, in fact, are his temple (see 1 Cor. 6:19). We can avoid needless pain by honoring God with our lives. He's given us plenty of guidance for doing that. By eating well, resting as God commands us to, and avoiding sexual immorality and harmful substances such as alcohol, tobacco, and illicit drugs, we greatly improve our enjoyment of life.

Along with that, relating to God and others honestly and lovingly will help us avoid spiritual and emotional suffering as well. When we confess sin, we're freed from guilt. When we follow Jesus' "Golden Rule" and treat others the way we'd like to be treated (see Luke 6:31), we have healthier relationships. The advice is simple but true: Life goes better when lived God's way.

Can you think of an instance when you brought pain upon yourself? What did you learn from the experience?

Be Honest

Next, be honest about your suffering. That involves first defining what suffering is and then distinguishing between genuine suffering and a simple interruption in an otherwise comfortable life.

Some of us seem to thrive on crises. It is as if life revolves around a series of painful events that we must patiently endure. Often, these "traumatic" events are just the routines of daily life—a traffic jam or a spoiled dinner. That's not suffering.

Real suffering does exist, however, even in the relative comfort of North American society. For some it is a chronic illness. For others it may be pain inflicted by abuse or neglect. For others it may be hurt brought on by their own doing, such as poor financial planning, damaging relationship choices, or destructive habits that result in failed health. Even self-inflicted suffering is real and painful, and it is important to Christ. So the next step in being honest about suffering is to be honest before God about your pain.

Psalm 22 shows that we are free to bring our pain before God in honest lamentation. It begins with the words that Jesus later spoke on the cross, "My God, my God, why have you forsaken me?" (22:1). David continued by painting a graphic picture of suffering and pain at the hands of the ungodly. Both David and Jesus used these words to pour out their pain before the Father. You can do the same.

What is the difference between suffering and inconvenience?

Trust God

Too often, we blame God for our pain rather than look to him for help and comfort. While God allows suffering, he is still good. It was human sin that initiated suffering. God remains willing to redeem us, even using suffering in the process.

When we suffer, our thoughts quickly center on ourselves and often take an accusatory tone toward God:

- Why is this happening to me?
- Is this what I get for trying to be good?
- If God cared about me, he'd never let this happen.

Rather than accuse God, simply admit your sorrow to him and seek his comfort, guidance, and relief. Christ's purpose in suffering was to redeem us. Our purpose is to be fully reconciled to him. Therefore the best result of suffering is that we would simply focus more of our attention on Christ.

Because we live in an instant age, we tend to believe that we should have an instant understanding of all that is happening to us. When we don't see immediate solutions, we become angry. But some things we simply will not understand until we get to heaven. In the meantime, we trust God—even when we suffer.

When we are pressed near to God's heart, he is faithful, and he will hold us. Jesus said, "Therefore I tell you, do not worry about your life, what you will eat or drink; or about your body, what you will wear" (Matt. 6:25). We can entrust our souls to the faithful Creator. Few feelings compare with the joy of watching God step in and solve a problem that seems impossible. When you suffer, ask for God's help, then wait for him to provide what is best—whether it's relief from suffering, an important lesson of faith, or simply the grace to endure.

During the short term, God is faithful, and we can depend upon him. When you are tempted to lose hope, remember that God has not abandoned you.

What would you say to a friend whose suffering has caused him or her to lose faith in God?

Focus on the Eternal

The truth that God is faithful does not necessarily mean that our suffering will quickly disappear. Our Lord's agenda for us is full of surprises and unexpected twists.

When we suffer, we may resist God's attempts to redirect our lives and look for ways to cope on our own. When trials linger and you begin to wear down, Satan will make all kinds of suggestions. He will even give you evidence that other people were able to run away from what you have to endure. He will call into question God's integrity. He'll point to many ways that you can avoid suffering by breaking faith with God.

When that happens, take the long view. Focus on the eternal glory that God has in store for us. God is busy with us, shaping us and using suffering as an instrument. The final goal for all of us is that we can be made into the image of our Lord Jesus Christ. The apostle Paul gave us this wonderful promise: "And we know that in all things God works for the good of those who love him, who have been called according to his purpose" (Rom. 8:28). Yet we need to hear the following verse as well: "For those God foreknew he also predestined to be conformed to the image of his Son" (8:29). The ultimate goal for every Christian is to become like Christ. Though there surely will be some progress toward that goal in this life, the final realization will occur in the endless ages that we will spend with him.

From time to time, all of us need to face the marvelous truth that this world is not our home. God is preparing us to live with the King of Kings and Lord of Lords. In a real sense, living here is a preparation for eternal life.

List some good things that may result from your suffering.

Reach Out

One way we can learn and thrive even in the midst of suffering is to elevate our vision beyond ourselves and our pain and to minister to others. Paul suggested that, because of his chains, many had turned to Christ. Can our "chains" have that same effect? Certainly not as long as we keep our focus on the chains themselves. The more we focus on ourselves, the more saturated our minds become with our own hurts and the less we are able to think of anything but our own plight.

If, however, we focus on the higher purpose to which we have been called in Christ, we can accomplish good things, even in our suffering!

Recall David's lamentation in Psalm 22. In verse 22, the poem takes a dramatic turn away from David's inner pain to express a sense of purpose and direction. As David looked at the wonders of God, he grew thankful. Finally, he exclaimed, "For he has not despised or scorned the suffering of the afflicted one; he has not hidden his face from him but has listened to his cry for help. From you comes the theme of my praise in the great assembly; before those who fear you I will fulfill my vows" (Ps. 22:24–25).

Is it possible that David discovered a purpose in suffering? Can you? When we concentrate on God and others instead of ourselves, we can find meaning in spite of our suffering.

Although we may not be able to change our circumstances, we can control our attitude toward them. As we cultivate a servant's attitude, we discover that suffering does not have the last word!

Name a way in which you might help another person in spite of what you have suffered—or because of it.

WEEK 5

CONSCIENCE AND CONVICTIONS

Religion that God our Father accepts as pure and faultless is this: to look after orphans and widows in their distress and to keep oneself from being polluted by the world.

—James 1:27

BIBLE BASICS

- James 1:19–27

When this Scripture was written, the care of widows and orphans was an important social issue. What are some pressing social or moral issues today? How might Christians address them?

LIVING BY CONSCIENCE

The world has changed a lot since Jesus walked the earth, but people and their problems are remarkably the same. Many of the issues our society faces were also present during the time of Christ. Christians still must determine how to live as God's children in an ungodly world. As we do that, biblical truth continues to be relevant.

What moral issues do you face in your own life? What ethical dilemmas must you wrestle with at work? What are the needs of our society? How can we believers in Jesus Christ make a difference in the world around us?

To answer these questions, you must first form your own convictions based on God's Word and the Holy Spirit's guidance. But you're not alone in that search. Christians have traditionally relied on one another when making important decisions about lifestyle and social issues. As a group, Wesleyans have sifted through many of our generation's pressing questions and developed a common response. We refer to that as our collective conscience or collective convictions.

John Wesley gave strong attention to the social ills of his day, including slavery and the need for prison reform. Those of us who are in the Wesleyan tradition continue to be greatly concerned about the problems people face in our world. We're eager to see God's transforming grace at work not only in us, but also in other people and in society as a whole. We want to make a difference in our world!

And that difference begins with individual believers like you.

FORMING YOUR OWN CONVICTIONS

Have you heard the saying, "God has many children but no grandchildren"? It means that your salvation cannot depend on the faith of others, including Christians of a previous generation. We each stand before God as individuals. The beliefs of other Christians may provide an important guide, but ultimately you must act according to your own conscience.

That's why no list of rules adequately protects us from all the world's evils or prompts us to do good in every possible way. Something surely would get left out, and we might be tempted to think that righteousness depends on learning a few dos and don'ts rather than on developing a right relationship with God. Although we value the church's guidance, it's really a cop-out to say, "I only do this (or don't do it) because the church says so." Real faith enables one to say, "I choose to live as I do because I believe it pleases Jesus Christ."

The apostle Paul gave some helpful guidelines for forming personal convictions when he wrote to young Timothy. He counseled, "Run from anything that gives you . . . evil thoughts . . . but stay close to anything that makes you want to do right. Have faith and love, and enjoy the companionship of those who love the Lord and have pure hearts" (2 Tim. 2:22 TLB).

Let's take a closer look at the principles expressed in that Scripture. As we do, keep in mind the elements of Wesley's Quadrilateral: Scripture, tradition, experience, and reason, and begin to form or strengthen your own convictions on the moral and social issues of our day.

Avoiding Evil

Godly living involves making conscious decisions to avoid evil. Evil is anything that is opposed to God or interferes with our relationship with him. It could be a philosophy, attitude, or lifestyle; or it could be an action, habit, recreation, or even a career. Evil is anything that robs us or those we influence of a fully enjoyable life in Christ. To live as Jesus lived requires that we identify evil in our lives and choose to avoid it.

Some forms of evil are obvious and therefore easy to identify. Things like greed and sexual immorality are clearly wrong. Many evils, however, are less clear. For instance, when does acquiring possessions change from being prudent to being materialistic? Where is the line between providing for one's family by working hard and neglecting one's family by working too much? You'll need the Holy Spirit's guidance to clarify these gray areas, but the Bible is clear in telling us to run from evil. When in doubt, it's best to avoid an attitude or action that has the potential to hinder your faithfulness.

The best way to overcome evil is to replace it with something good. As we develop perfect love for God and others, evil thoughts, habits, and associations will begin to fall away.

Choosing What's Good

Godly living involves making intentional choices that fill our lives with whatever draws us closer to God. Evil aborts, cripples, and kills life in Christ. Good things enrich that life. We should choose to do things that increase our love for the Lord and our ability to share that love with others. Thoughts, actions, and associations that strengthen our minds, nourish our faith, and improve our moral judgment should be made into habits.

There are more dos than don'ts in the Christian life. As Jesus said, "If the Son sets you free, you will be free indeed" (John 8:36). Sin is slavery of the will. Knowing the Lord opens the door to abundant living. Jesus gives us freedom to say no to sin and yes to things that are good, holy, and uplifting.

Putting Others First

Godly living involves placing the spiritual welfare of others ahead of our own satisfaction. Putting other people first is another way of saying we love them.

For Christians that practice begins in one's spiritual home, the church. How can we love our enemies, as Jesus expects us to, if we don't love our brothers and sisters in the faith? A thoroughly Christian lifestyle leads to deeper fellowship with others who love the Lord and have pure hearts. Mature believers, therefore, are willing to surrender some of their own rights in order to advance the spiritual welfare of other Christians.

Some Christian convictions involve gray areas, those matters of conscience that may easily become stumbling blocks to other Christians (meaning they could offend or otherwise spiritually hurt them). When deciding whether some action is appropriate, consider the effect it might have on others. Even if you feel freedom in a certain area, if it might adversely affect other Christians, why do it? (See Rom. 14:1—15:13 for more on this point.)

Putting others first also means that we want to serve and witness to nonbelievers. For that reason, Christians have always been involved in correcting society's evils and ministering to the needy. Providing medical care and education, advocating prison reform, feeding the hungry, providing shelter for the homeless, promoting the abolition of slavery, and supporting the temperance movement are some of the ways Christians throughout history have put love into action. We make a difference in the world!

What are the needs of people in your community, and how can you help meet them?

COLLECTIVE CONVICTIONS

Every Christian is guided by his or her own conscience on matters of personal conviction. Yet there's a value in taking a common approach to many social issues. We believe that the Holy Spirit speaks to the church as well as to individual believers, and the affirmation of the body gives us greater confidence in our convictions.

ELEMENTARY PRINCIPLES

Certain shared beliefs that form the basis of our thinking on a number of contemporary issues are referred to as "Elementary Principles." Here are the Elementary Principles of The Wesleyan Church.[1]

- Christ is the only Head of the church, and the Word of God the only rule of faith and conduct.
- No person who loves the Lord Jesus Christ, and obeys the gospel of God our Savior, ought to be deprived of church membership.
- Every person has an inalienable right to private judgment in matters of religion and an equal right to express personal opinions in any way which will not violate the laws of God or the rights of others.
- All church trials should be conducted on gospel principles only; and no minister or member should be excommunicated except for immorality, the propagation of unchristian doctrines, or for neglect of duties enjoined by the Word of God.
- The pastoral or ministerial office and duties are of divine appointment, and all ordained ministers in the church of God are

equal; but ministers are forbidden to be lords over God's heritage or to have dominion over the faith of the saints.

- The Church has a right to form and enforce such rules and regulations only as are in accordance with the Holy Scriptures and may be necessary or have a tendency to carry into effect the great system of practical Christianity.
- Whatever power may be necessary to the formation of rules and regulations is inherent in the ministers and members of the church; but so much of that power may be delegated from time to time, upon a plan of representation, as they may judge necessary and proper.
- It is the duty of all ministers and members of the Church to maintain godliness and oppose all moral evil.
- It is obligatory upon ministers of the gospel to be faithful in the discharge of their pastoral and ministerial duties, and it is also obligatory upon the members to esteem ministers highly for the works' sake, and to render them a righteous compensation for their labors.

SOCIAL ISSUES

The Wesleyan Church was born in a society that had many evils. Early Wesleyans had the courage not only to speak out about them, but also to pursue social changes, including the abolition of slavery and the ordination of women. We continue to believe that Christians should engage the culture, witnessing, teaching, and acting in ways that bring about positive social change.

Based on this conviction, collective statements on many of the important issues of our day are referred to as "Special Directions" and are intended as a guide for churches and believers on the vital issues of our society. Here are some of the Special Directions of The Wesleyan Church.

Racism

We vigorously oppose the denial of basic human and civil rights to any individual due to their race, gender, or national origin. We admit that, while our denomination was born in an antislavery movement, we ourselves have sometimes ignored our own heritage and been guilty of both personal and collective racism and prejudice. For this sin, we collectively repent today and ask for God's forgiveness, and we intend to strive for complete racial reconciliation, for we know that this is the will of God.

Related Scriptures: Psalm 139:13–16; Proverbs 22:2; Matthew 22:37–39; John 4:9; Acts 10:9–16, 28; 17:26; Romans 2:9–11; Galatians 3:28; James 2:1–4; 1 John 2:29—3:2; Revelation 5:9–10; 7:9.

Women in Leadership

In spite of some forces which seek to undo our long-standing position on the ordination of women, we refuse to budge on this issue. We will not tolerate the blocking of a person's ordination due to their gender, for we believe that both men and women are called to the ministry and thus should be ordained. Furthermore, we condemn any practice of exclusive, male-only leadership on boards and committees in the church, excluding women from those positions by either public policy or unofficial behind-the-scenes policy, for we believe that when it comes to God's gifts, graces, and callings, there is neither male nor female.

Related Scriptures: books of Esther and Ruth; Galatians 3:28.

Political Action

While we do not place our hope in political action and partisan politics, but in God alone, we do recognize that North American society is crumbling morally and culturally. We call upon all political parties to cease their petty bickering, position posturing, and political one-upmanship, and get about the task of rebuilding a strong, God-fearing civilization where the poor receive compassionate care, criminals are punished, governments live within their means, the next generation is educated with wisdom, and trust in God comes to the core of our culture.

Related Scriptures: Matthew 22:21; Acts 5:29; Romans 13:1–7; Titus 3:1.

Abuse

We condemn sexual, physical, emotional, and verbal abuse by all persons everywhere, but especially abuse perpetrated by members of a family or a church community. We commit ourselves to provide safe havens for the abused victims among us and to seek out and prosecute guilty offenders. While we understand there are differing interpretations among us of the Bible's teaching on the role of husband and wife in the home, we totally reject any exercise of abuse by one spouse of another by twisting these Scriptures out of context. Such abuse is sin and the sinner should be called to repent and cease all such abusive behavior.

Related Scriptures: Proverbs 29:22; Ecclesiastes 7:9; 1 Corinthians 13; 1 John 3:15.

Marriage and Sexual Purity

We have witnessed a general decline of our culture's standards on both divorce and premarital sexual activity, but we reaffirm that divorce is a sin, sexual intercourse before marriage is a sin, and sexual intercourse with anyone except one's spouse after marriage is likewise a sin. In a day of easy divorce, we continue to stand firmly on the Bible's teaching that God's plan for marriage is for one man and one woman together for one entire life and that sexual immorality is one possible reason for divorce (in addition to spousal abuse), and only then after serious spiritual counsel. We further call our members to flee from any dangerous relationships fraught with temptations toward a level of sexual intimacy short of actual intercourse, which are totally improper for God's holy people.

While others may compromise on matters of divorce, premarital and extramarital sex, we affirm the sinfulness of these behaviors and call on ourselves to treat a sinner in each case with loving confrontation, a call to repentance, forgiveness, and restoration.

Related Scriptures: Genesis 2:18, 24; Malachi 2:14; Matthew 19:5, 9; 1 Corinthians 6:18–20; 7:12–15; Ephesians 5:22—6:4.

Abortion

We believe that abortion is the taking of human life; therefore, society brings grave danger to itself by permitting abortion on demand and thus treating God-given life so lightly. We call our members to oppose this social evil with great vigor. However, we reject the use of violence as a means of bringing about this needed change in society. Except in the case of risk to the life of the mother, The Wesleyan Church stands firm against the evil of abortion—both the personal evil of abortion by any individual among us and the worldwide social evil of abortion, which we believe must someday end. Until that day, we will instruct our people to avoid this sin personally and call them to the work of enlightening a blind culture, as we once did with the sin of slavery.

Related Scriptures: Genesis 1:26–27; 2:7; Psalm 8:5; 119:73; 127:3; 139:13–14; Isaiah 44:2; 46:3.

Homosexuality

While we believe God loves—and we should also love—all sinners, including adulterers, fornicators, as well as those who practice homosexuality—we specifically reaffirm our strong position that the practice of homosexuality is a sin, and that even the propensity toward homosexuality is out of step with both the order of creation and the will of God. On this matter we cannot and will not compromise—the only marriage blessed by God is a lifelong commitment between one man and one woman. Those practicing homosexuality should be treated like any other sinner—with love and concern, yet with a call to repentance and conversion through God's grace which results in the cessation of sinful behavior.

Related Scriptures: Leviticus 18:22; 20:13; Matthew 9:36, 14:14; Mark 1:41; Romans 1:27.

Substance Abuse

Wesleyans have traditionally stood against all substance abuse such as the use of tobacco, alcohol, and other drugs. While we understand the biological and psychological nature of addictions, we affirm that God's grace is powerful enough to deliver any sincere believer from slavery to any of these substances. Furthermore, we believe that the sale and trafficking of tobacco, alcohol, and other nonmedical drugs is a social evil which is draining and corrupting to society, and thus we believe that the best position is to practice total abstinence, protesting both the legal and illegal trade of such substances.

Related Scriptures: 1 Corinthians 6:20; 10:21; Galatians 5:16, 19–21.

Holy living is the hallmark of Wesleyan identity. Holiness is not only a doctrine but also a lifestyle: it calls us to confront the evils of our world and to engage in the appropriate means to bring about positive changes. We believe in becoming better people and in making the world a better place!

What is the biggest social issue facing your community? How can you help to address that issue?

NOTE

1. *The Discipline of The Wesleyan Church 2012* (Indianapolis, IN: Wesleyan Publishing House, 2012), 27–28.

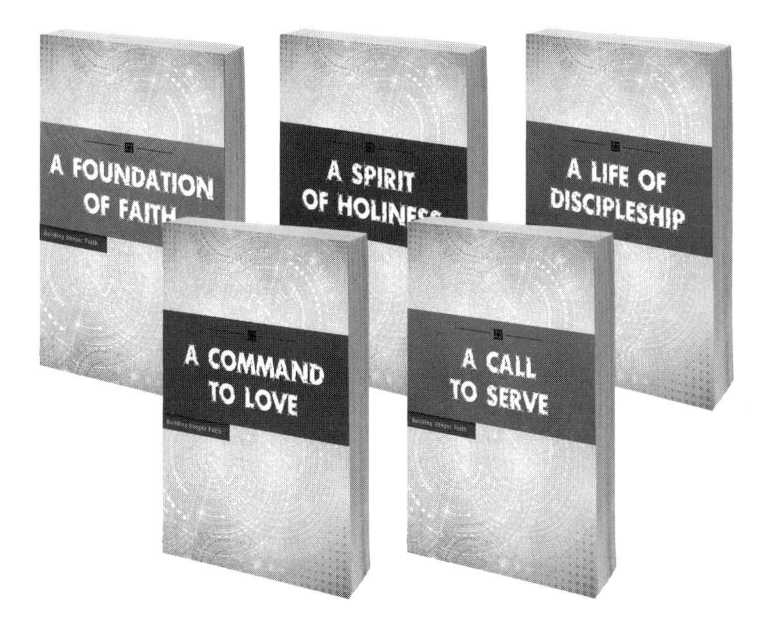